Rock Climbing
Making It to the Top

by Cynthia A. Dean

Reading Consultant:
Timothy Rasinski, Ph.D.
Professor of Reading Education
Kent State University

Content Consultant:
Andy Bourne
Mountain Guide
American Alpine Institute

Red Brick™ Learning

Published by Red Brick™ Learning
7825 Telegraph Road, Bloomington, Minnesota 55438
http://www.redbricklearning.com

Library of Congress Cataloging-in-Publication Data
Dean, Cynthia A., 1970–
    Rock climbing: making it to the top / by Cynthia A. Dean;
    reading consultant, Timothy Rasinski.
        p. cm.—(High five reading)
    Includes bibliographical references and index.
    ISBN 0-7368-5745-1 (soft cover)—ISBN 0-7368-5735-4 (hard cover)
    1. Rock climbing—United States—Juvenile literature. 2. Rock climbing for
children—United States—Juvenile literature. I. Rasinski, Timothy V. II.
Title. III. Series.
GV199.4.D42 2006
796.52'23—dc22
                                2005010401

Created by Kent Publishing Services, Inc.
Designed by Signature Design Group, Inc.
Edited by Jerry Ruff, Managing Editor, Red Brick™ Learning
Red Brick™ Learning Editorial Director: Mary Lindeen

This publisher has made every effort to trace ownership of all copyrighted
material and to secure necessary permissions. In the event of any questions
arising as to the use of any material, the publisher, while expressing regret for
any inadvertent error, will be happy to make necessary corrections.

Photo Credits:
Cover, Alan Mounic/Fep/Panoramic, Zuma Press; pages 4, 8 bottom, 10, 11
(top and middle), 13, 15, 21, 22, 24, 29, Dan Patitucci, PatitucciPhoto;
page 6, Hulton Archive/Corbis; pages 8 (top), 9, 11 (bottom), 12, Corbis;
pages 16, 19, Roberto Fioravanti; page 23, Jerry Dodrill, Dodrill Gallery; pages
26, 30, Heinz Zak; page 33, Roger L. Wollenberg, UPI Photo Service; page 34,
Tony Donaldson, Icon SMI; pages 36, 39, Associated Press, A/P

Many climbers featured in this book are shown not wearing helmets. The
publisher does not endorse the lack of safety equipment while rock climbing.

Printed in the United States of America.

1 2 3 4 5 6 11 10 09 08 07 06 05

Table of Contents

Chris Sharma grips a handhold during a climb.

CHAPTER 1

What Is Rock Climbing?

*His body swings across the rock. He seems to hang in the air. He grabs a piece of rock with two fingers. The **handhold** is no bigger than an apple.*
For a moment, just two fingers keep him from falling!

America's "Rock" Star

Chris Sharma is a rock climber. Right now, he is 150 feet (46 meters) off the ground! You might call Chris a "rock" star!

In this book, you will meet several great climbers. You will also learn several ways to rock climb. But first, just what is rock climbing?

---

handhold (HAND-hohld): a piece of rock a climber holds on to

Climbing in the Past

People first climbed hills and mountains just to get places. Also, from high up they could see farther. In the 1700s, people began to climb mountains for sport. Some people rock climbed to practice for mountain climbing. Later, rock climbing became a sport, too.

In the past, people might climb mountains to learn more about the land and weather.

Types of Rock Climbing

Today, there are seven types of rock climbing:

- Traditional
- Sport
- Aid
- Big Wall
- Bouldering
- Speed
- Indoor

In this book, you will learn something about each type. You will also meet some climbers who can really "rock"!

Let's Get Started

So let's get started. First, you will need tools. You will also need to learn **techniques**. Then you will be ready for the seven types of climbing.

---

technique (tek-NEEK): a way of doing something that takes skill

Rock Climbing Gear

You will need many tools to rock climb. Some tools help you climb. Others keep you safe. Take a look.

Shoes—Rock climbing shoes have sticky rubber soles. These shoes help climbers grip the rock as they climb.

Chalk Bag—Climbers use chalk on their hands. Chalk dries up sweat. Dry hands grip rock better than sweaty hands. The bag holds the chalk.

Helmet—A helmet **protects** a climber's head in a fall. It also protects a climber's head from falling rocks.

Harness—A **nylon** harness fits around a climber's waist and thighs. A climbing rope can be tied to this harness.

Rope—Climbing rope is also made of nylon. Climbers use this strong rope to go up and down a rock.

---

protect (pruh-TEKT): to keep something from harm
nylon (NYE-lon): a strong, plastic fiber used to make rope

Belay Device—Climbers use a belay (beh-LAY) device to hold and control the rope as they climb.

Nut—Climbers place nuts into cracks in rocks. The nut head fills the crack. Nuts have a wire cord on one end. Climbers hook into this cord as they climb. Climbers can remove nuts as they climb.

device (di-VISE): a tool that does a certain job

Bolt and Bolt Hanger—

Climbers may place bolts into holes they drill in rock. Each bolt has a hanger. Climbers can hook into the hangers as they climb. Bolts cannot be removed like nuts can.

Bolt hanger

Cam—

Cams work like nuts, except cams have a spring. The spring makes the cam head wider to fill cracks. Climbers hook into cam cords as they climb. Cams also can be removed.

Carabiner—

Climbers use carabiners (CAR-ah-BIN-erz) to hook tools to their harness. Climbers also hook carabiners into nut cords, cam cords, and bolt hangers as they climb.

Top Roping

Okay, you have your climbing tools. Now let's learn two ways to rock climb safely. These are top roping and lead climbing.

To top rope, tie one end of your climbing rope to your harness. This rope also must pass through an **anchor** at the top of your climb. Below you, a belayer holds the other end of your rope. The belayer keeps the rope tight as you climb. Top roping is safe and a good way to learn to climb.

A belayer holds the rope in top roping.

anchor (ANG-kur): a bolt hanger that is attached to the rock

Lead Climbing

To lead climb, you lead, or carry, the
rope up as you climb. As you climb higher,
you clip the rope into nuts, cams, or bolt
hangers. Each time you clip the rope, you
make yourself safe from a fall.

*The climber above is lead climbing. The second
climber, below, will follow him up the rock face.*

Getting Down

Climbers walk down from the top of some climbs. Not all climbs have a safe way to walk down, though. You need to check this out ahead of time.

Lowering

If you top roped, your belayer will lower you down. Don't forget to lean back. This will pull the rope tight. Your belayer will slowly let the rope pass through the belay device. Down you come!

Rappelling

To rappel (rah-PEL), use the rope that goes through your belay device. This same rope also must go through an anchor at the top of your climb. Use your belay device to control how fast you come down. The photo on page 15 shows a climber rappelling.

This climber is rappelling down a rock face.

America's Best Climbers

Now you know a little about climbing.
It's time to meet some "rock" stars.
Some of their climbs will amaze you!

Chris Sharma climbs Realization.

— CHAPTER **2** —

Sport, Traditional, and Aid Climbing

Chris Sharma had just climbed 66 feet (20 meters).
He was about halfway up the rock and very tired!
*But there was no place to rest. He **wedged** his feet*
*against the **rock face**. Any slip and he could fall!*
He asked his body to push harder.

The Toughest Sport Climb

Realization (ree-ah-lye-ZAY-shuhn) is the
toughest sport climb on Earth. It is part of
a large cliff in France. Realization is 120 feet
(37 meters) tall. Chris Sharma had climbed
66 feet (20 meters) without a rest.

---

wedge (WEJ): to force or press something into a small space
rock face (ROK FAYSS): the surface of a large piece of rock
or cliff

17

Climbing Realization

Chris Sharma wanted to **scale** Realization.
Many climbers before him had tried.
All had failed. Then, Chris gave it a try.
In fact, he gave it 30 tries. Each time, he
also failed.

One More Try

On July 18, 1999, Chris tried Realization
for the 31st time. At times, he lost his grip
on the rock face and slipped. When the
rope stopped his fall, he hit hard against
the rocks. But he kept on trying.

Then, after just 18 minutes, he made it!
Chris had climbed the hardest sport climb
in the world!

Do you want to learn to sport climb?
Read on to learn how.

---

scale (SKALE): to climb up something

"I love climbing. It's a great way to be in nature," says Chris Sharma.

Sport Climbing

To sport climb, you follow a set path up a rock face. To protect yourself from a fall, you clip into bolt hangers as you climb.

Usually you sport climb on almost **vertical** rock faces. These "straight up" rock faces make climbing very hard. Sport climbing tests your strength.

---

vertical (VUR-tuh-kuhl): upright, or straight up and down

Sport climbers use chalk on their hands to help them hold on to the rock.

Traditional Climbing

Rock climbing began with traditional climbing. For this type of free climb, you find your own way up a rock. You don't follow a line of bolts. Your hands and feet are your main tools. As you go up, you clip your rope into nuts or cams to keep you from falling.

Climbers use only their hands and feet when traditional climbing.

Aid Climbing

Some rock faces cannot be climbed using only hands and feet. For these, you might aid climb. One way to aid climb is to use aiders. You clip these aiders into cams, nuts, or bolt hangers. Then you step on aiders to go higher.

Do you want to learn about some more climbs? How about one where you sleep high up on a rock wall?

This climber is using aiders to move up the rock.

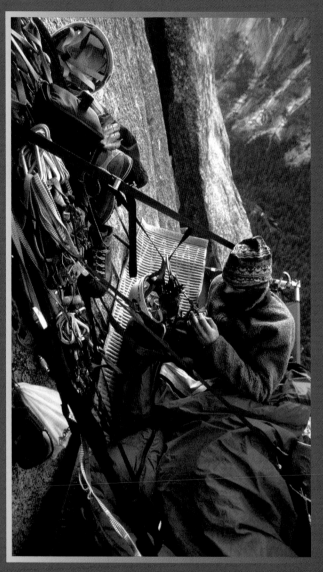

Big wall climbers often spend days climbing a single rock wall. They eat and sleep on the rock wall.

CHAPTER 3

Big Wall Climbing and Bouldering

You free climb up a giant wall of rock. There are no bolts or nuts to hang on to. Suddenly, your foot slips. You fall! But your rope stops you. You are more than 2,000 feet (610 meters) above the ground below!

Big Wall Climbing

You need to rest after the fall. You know it will take days to reach the top. You will eat and even sleep on the face of the rock. As you are resting you ask yourself, "Why am I doing this?"

But really, you know why you do it. You big wall climb to test your strength. You want to be out in nature. You enjoy the peace and quiet out on a rock.

El Capitan

In 1994, Lynn Hill became the first person to free climb The Nose. The Nose is part of a huge rock called El Capitan (EL ca-pee-TAHN). El Capitan is located in Yosemite (yoh-SEH-meh-tee) National Park, California. Lynn made this climb in less than a day.

Lynn Hill uses only her hands and feet to climb under The Great Roof on The Nose of El Capitan.

The Hardest Free Climb

Lynn's climb wasn't easy. The late summer heat made it too hot to start in the day. So, Lynn started at 10:00 p.m. She climbed by moonlight.

At 2,000 feet (610 meters), Lynn reached a large chunk of rock that hangs over the rock wall. Climbers call this rock The Great Roof. By 10:25 a.m., Lynn had made it past The Great Roof.

Time to Rest

Lynn still had 1,000 feet (305 meters) to climb to the top of The Nose. She waited for the sun to set. At 5:30 p.m., the rock face was cooler in the shade. Lynn started again. She fell twice. Each time, her rope stopped her fall. After a third fall, Lynn knew she had to rest. Would she make it?

Reaching the Top

Finally, Lynn climbed by lamplight. At the top of the climb, she held on by two fingers. Pulling herself up, Lynn reached the top. It took 23 hours, but she had free climbed The Nose!

Bouldering

If you are not ready for big wall climbing, you might like bouldering. Bouldering is done close to the ground. You don't need a rope for bouldering. For safety, you use a team of **spotters**. Spotters place a crash pad below you. If you fall, the pad gives you a soft place to land.

---

spotter (SPAH-tuhr): someone who watches another climber in case she or he falls

Speedsters

For some climbers, speed is what it's all about. The best speed climbers can scramble up a rock wall in less than 14 seconds. Do you have a need for speed?

This woman is bouldering. There is a crash pad below her.

Dean Potter speed climbs up Half Dome.

CHAPTER 4

Speed and Indoor Climbing

The goal is speed. A 3,000-foot (914-meter) climb stands before you. You start your watch. "Go! Go!" You race up the rock. Five minutes later, you are 200 feet (61 meters) up the rock face.

Speed Climbing

Speed climbing is a race. You want to be first to the top of a climb. You can speed climb both indoors and outdoors. You can compete alone or as a team.

The rules for team speed climbing are simple. The clock starts when the first person on your team starts to climb. The clock stops when the last person on the team makes it to the top.

Indoor Climbing

Indoor climbing is the safest way to climb. Indoor climbers scale an **artificial** rock wall. Many indoor climbing gyms offer climbing classes. In fact, most people rock climb for the first time indoors.

These climbers are speed climbing on an artificial wall.

artificial (ar-ti-FISH-uhl): not real or natural

33

Tori Allen—Teen Rocket

Tori Allen first climbed at age 10. Since then, Tori has "rocked" at speed climbing. Tori is strong. She can do pull-ups with one finger!

Tori won an adult speed-climbing event at her first X-Games in 2002. She climbed a 60-foot (18-meter) wall in less than 14 seconds! Not bad for a 14-year-old!

Tori Allen competes at the 2002 X-Games.

Dean Potter—King of Yosemite

In September 2002, speed climber Dean Potter reached the top of his sport. He aid climbed and free climbed Yosemite's two best-known rock faces—El Capitan and Half Dome. That's a total of 4,900 feet (1,494 meters)—almost a mile up!

But amazingly, Dean climbed both rocks without a break—and he did it in less than a day! El Capitan and Half Dome each take **average** climbers three or more days to climb.

How to Get Started

Would you like to try rock climbing? In the next chapter, learn where, when, and how you can get started.

---

average (AV-uh-rij): usual or ordinary

People of all ages are taking up the sport of rock climbing.

CHAPTER 5

Where Can I Climb?

Rock climbing is fun. It's easy, too. You can learn how to rock climb in a day. You can climb indoors or outdoors. Rock climbing also gives you a new way to work out. So where can you go to rock climb?

Rocking North America

There are many places to rock climb in the United States and Canada. One place is at a rock climbing camp. There, you can learn from the best, like Chris Sharma. You can also sign up for a class at a climbing gym. Tori Allen teaches a climbing class at her gym.

Are you ready to go rock climbing? Where would you like to climb first?

Climbing in the United States

There are many places to go rock climbing in the United States. Some good ones are in California, Oregon, Nevada, and Colorado.

California has some of the best rock climbing in the world. One top spot is Yosemite Valley in Yosemite National Park.

Scaling Smith Rock

Smith Rock in Oregon is best known for its sport climbs. **Volcanic** rocks fill this desert area. Smith Rock has cliffs and rock towers of many colors.

---

volcanic (vol-KAN-ik): of or from a volcano

Rocking Red Rocks

In Nevada, Red Rocks is the place for long, free-climbing routes. Sandstone **crags** and **canyons** cut into the desert at Red Rocks. Here, it is best to climb in spring or fall when the weather isn't too hot.

Red Rocks, Nevada, is a great place to climb.

crag (KRAG): a steep, sharp rock or cliff
canyon (KAN-yuhn): a deep, narrow river valley with steep sides

Climbing in Canada

Canada has many places to go rock climbing as well. In fact, every **province** in Canada has places to rock climb.

Rock Climbing the Rockies

In the Canadian Rockies, teens can learn to rock climb. Climbers are taught both sport and traditional climbing. Some climbs are long and have many **pitches**. Climbers 13 to 17 can join in the fun.

province (PROV-uhnss): a district or region of a country
pitch (PICH): one rope length

Beating Old Baldy

The mountains around Niagara Falls have many sport climbs. These limestone climbs are no more than 80 feet (24 meters) high. Old Baldy, north of Toronto, is one of Canada's best sport climbing spots.

Find a Climbing Gym Near You

There are many climbing gyms in North America. For a list of climbing gyms, go to:

www.indoorclimbing.com/northamericangyms.html

Epilogue

"Rock" Talk

Like most sports, rock climbing has its own language. Here are some words and phrases that rock climbers use.

Barn Door—When a climber loses the footholds and handholds on one side of the body. This makes the climber swing out from the rock like a barn door opening.

Bivy—To sleep outside without a tent; short for the word *bivouac*

Brain Bucket—Another name for a helmet

Bucket—A large handhold to hang on to; also called a *jug*

Cheese Grater—When a climber scrapes knees, hands, and face while sliding down a rock

Chickenheads—Rocks sticking out of a rock face that a climber hangs on to

Crater—To fall a long way and hit the ground hard enough to make a hole or "crater"

Crimper—A small handhold only big enough for fingertips

Flash—To lead a climb without falling on the first try

Gumbie—A new rock climber

Gym Rat—An indoor climber

Manky—Any old, loose, or rusted bolts or rocks on the rock face

Screamer—A fall long enough to give the climber time to scream out

Sewing-machine Leg—When a climber's leg starts to jump up and down because the muscle is tired or weak; also called "Elvis Syndrome"

Whipper—A long fall where the rope snaps the climber into the air during the fall

Wired—To know exactly how to climb a rock face

Glossary

anchor (ANG-kur): a bolt hanger that is attached to the rock

artificial (ar-ti-FISH-uhl): not real or natural

average (AV-uh-rij): usual or ordinary

canyon (KAN-yuhn): a deep, narrow river valley with steep sides

crag (KRAG): a steep, sharp rock or cliff

device (di-VISE): a tool that does a certain job

handhold (HAND-hohld): a piece of rock a climber holds on to

nylon (NYE-lon): a strong, plastic fiber used to make rope

pitch (PICH): one rope length

protect (pruh-TEKT): to keep something from harm

province (PROV-uhnss): a district or region of a country

rock face (ROK FAYSS): the surface of a large piece of rock or cliff

scale (SKALE): to climb up something

spotter (SPAH-tuhr): someone who watches another climber in case she or he falls

technique (tek-NEEK): a way of doing something that takes skill

vertical (VUR-tuh-kuhl): upright, or straight up and down

volcanic (vol-KAN-ik): of or from a volcano

wedge (WEJ): to force or press something into a small space

Bibliography

Deady, Kathleen. *Extreme Rock Climbing Moves.* Behind the Moves. Mankato, Minn.: Capstone Press, 2003.

Oxlade, Chris. *Rock Climbing.* Extreme Sports. Minneapolis: Lerner Publications, 2004.

Weintraub, Aileen. *Rock Climbing.* X-Treme Outdoors. New York: Children's Press, 2003.

Young, Ian. *X Games: Action Sports Grab the Spotlight.* High Five Reading. Bloomington, Minn.: Red Brick Learning, 2003.

Useful Addresses

The Alpine Club of Canada
P.O. Box 8040
Indian Flats Road
Canmore, Alberta T1W 2T8

The American Safe Climbing Association
P.O. Box 1814
Bishop, CA 93515

Internet Sites

The Alpine Club of Canada
www.alpineclubofcanada.ca/contacts/index.html

American Alpine Institute
http://www.aai.cc

The American Safe Climbing Association
http://www.safeclimbing.org/index.htm

indoorclimbing.com
http://www.indoorclimbing.com/
northamericangyms.html

Yamnuska (Rock climbing in Canada)
http://www.yamnuska.com/rockclimbing.html

Yo! Basecamp (Rock climbing camps for children
and adults in the United States)
http://www.yobasecamp.com

Index